Danger!

A Children's Book about Handling Fear, Dangerous Things, Places, and Situations

by

Joy Wilt

Illustrated by Ernie Hergenroeder

Educational Products Division
Word, Incorporated
Waco, Texas

Author

JOY WILT is creator and director of Children's Ministries, an organization that provides resources "for people who care about children"—speakers, workshops, demonstrations, consulting services, and training institutes. A certified elementary school teacher, administrator, and early childhood specialist, Joy is also consultant to and professor in the master's degree program in children's ministries for Fuller Theological Seminary. Joy is a graduate of LaVerne College, LaVerne, California (B.A. in Biological Science), and Pacific Oaks College, Pasadena, California (M.A. in Human Development). She is author of three books, *Happily Ever After*, *An Uncomplicated Guide to Becoming a Superparent*, and *Taming the Big Bad Wolves*, as well as the popular *Can-Make-And-Do Books*. Joy's commitment "never to forget what it feels like to be a child" permeates the many innovative programs she has developed and her work as lecturer, consultant, writer, and—not least—mother of two children, Christopher and Lisa.

Artist

ERNIE HERGENROEDER is founder and owner of Hergie & Associates (a visual communications studio and advertising agency). With the establishment of this company in 1975, "Hergie" and his wife, Faith, settled in San Jose with their four children, Lynn, Kathy, Stephen, and Beth. Active in community and church affairs, Hergie is involved in presenting creative workshops for teachers, ministers, and others who wish to understand the techniques of communicating visually. He also lectures in high schools to encourage young artists toward a career in commercial art. Hergie serves as a consultant to organizations such as the Police Athletic League (PAL), Girl Scouts, and religious and secular corporations. His ultimate goal is to touch the hearts of kids (8 to 80) all over the world—visually!

ISBN: 0-8499-8135-2
Library of Congress Catalog Card Number: 79-50044

Janet Gray, Editor

Contents

Introduction

<u>Danger!</u> is one of a series of books. The complete set is called *Ready-Set-Grow!*

<u>Danger!</u> deals with handling fear, dangerous things, places, and situations, and can be used by itself or as a part of a program that utilizes all of the *Ready-Set-Grow!* books.

<u>Danger!</u> is specifically designed so that children can either read the book themselves or have it read to them. This can be done at home, church, or school. When reading to children, it is not necessary to complete the book at one sitting. Concern should be given to the attention span of the individual child and his or her comprehension of the subject matter.

<u>Danger!</u> is designed to involve the child in concepts that are being taught. This is done by simply and carefully explaining each concept and then asking questions that invite a response from the child. It is hoped that by answering the questions, the child will personalize the concept and, thus, integrate it into his or her thinking.

<u>Danger!</u> teaches that each child is an important person and therefore must do everything possible to keep from harm. To avoid harm, children need to understand and gain control of their fears, dangerous things, dangerous places, and dangerous situations.

Fear is an unpleasant and often embarrassing emotion, but it can be a warning of danger. Through questions, the book invites the child to confront his or her fears.

Danger! is designed to help children understand when their fears are irrational—and when they are wise. Although many situations, places, and things are inherently dangerous, children can often learn a great deal from them—so the book presents guidelines for dealing with them safely.

Children have a need and a desire to learn, and they learn best from their own experience. This is what makes it hard for them to have a thing, place, or situation labeled an unqualified "no-no!" by adults who merely care about their safety.

God created and loves each person, and wants us to love ourselves. One way we do this is by keeping ourselves safe from harm, but another way is by allowing ourselves to continue growing and learning, which we cannot do if we are enslaved by our fears. Children who grow up learning how to deal intelligently with their fears and to cope with dangerous things, places, and situations will be better equipped to live healthy, productive lives.

6

Danger!

You are an important person, and because you are . . .

you need to take good care of yourself.

You must not do anything that will harm you.

You must do everything you can to make sure nothing harms you.

To avoid harm, you need to understand:

> your fears,
> dangerous things,
> dangerous places, and
> dangerous situations.

This book can help you.

Chapter 1

Handling Fear

This is Hilary. Hilary is afraid of animals, especially strange and wild ones. She is afraid they might hurt her.

This is Joseph. Joseph is afraid of being alone. He's not sure he can take care of himself and protect himself when he is alone.

This is Star. Star is afraid a burglar, kidnapper, or murderer might come and get her.

This is Melody. Melody is afraid of getting lost. She doesn't know what would happen to her if she got lost.

This is Jack. Jack is afraid something might hurt his body. Jack hates pain, and he doesn't want anything to happen to his body that would stop it from working right.

I DON'T THINK I WANT THIS BIKE. IF I TRY TO RIDE IT, I MIGHT FALL OFF AND HURT MYSELF REAL BAD!

This is Janet. Janet is afraid of change. She doesn't want things to become different from the way they are. This is because she doesn't know what it would be like if things changed.

This is Donald. Donald is afraid of the dark, because he can't
see if something is nearby that could hurt him.

This is Frank. Frank is afraid of death. He doesn't want to leave the people he loves. He doesn't know what dying feels like, and he doesn't want to do anything he doesn't understand. He's afraid dying might hurt.

This is Cindy. Cindy is afraid of high places. She's afraid she might fall and hurt herself.

This is Philip. Philip is afraid of large things. He thinks that if anything bigger than he tried to hurt him, he wouldn't be able to stop it.

This is Diane. Diane is afraid of losing someone she loves, such as her parents, her brother or sister, or a friend. Diane depends on these people and she doesn't know what would happen to her if they weren't there.

This is Jim. Jim is afraid of loud noises. He thinks the things that make loud sounds might come and hurt him. **27**

This is Frances. Frances is afraid of natural phenomena, such as wind, rain, thunder, and lightning. She doesn't understand them, and she's afraid she can't keep them from hurting her.

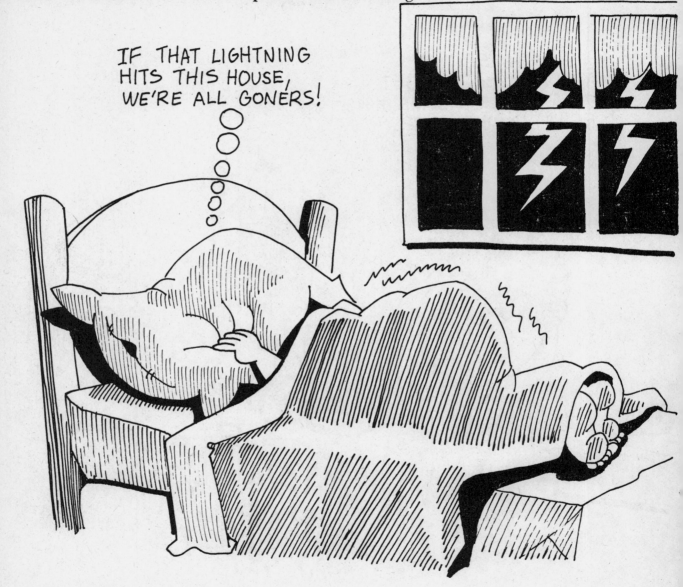

This is Steve. Steve is afraid of being separated from his family and friends. He depends on them and doesn't know what will happen to him when they aren't around.

This is Chuck. Chuck is afraid of supernatural beings, such as ghosts, goblins, witches, and monsters. Grownups have told him these things don't really exist, but he's heard stories and seen movies about them. He's sure that if they do exist, they hurt and kill people.

This is Connie. Connie is afraid of people she doesn't know. This is because she doesn't know if they will be nice to her or hurt her.

This is Patrick. Patrick is afraid of unfamiliar places, because he doesn't know what will happen to him there. He doesn't know how he will act or what the other people there will do to him.

This is Susan. Susan is afraid of the water. She's afraid she might get hurt in the water, or even drown.

Hilary is afraid of animals.

Joseph is afraid of being alone.

Star is afraid of being hurt or killed by someone.

Melody is afraid of getting lost.

Jack is afraid of hurting himself.

Janet is afraid of change.

Donald is afraid of the dark.

Frank is afraid of death.

Cindy is afraid of high places.

Philip is afraid of large things.

Diane is afraid of losing someone she loves.

Jim is afraid of loud noises.

Frances is afraid of natural phenomena.

Steve is afraid of being separated from his family and friends.

Chuck is afraid of supernatural beings.

Connie is afraid of people she doesn't know.

Patrick is afraid of unfamiliar places.

Susan is afraid of the water.

What about you?

Are you afraid of anything?

3 FT.

Are you afraid of any of these things?

Animals

Being alone

Being hurt or killed by someone

Getting lost

Hurting yourself

Change

The dark

Death

High places and falling

Large things

Losing someone you love

Loud noises

Natural phenomena

Being separated from your family and friends

Supernatural beings

People you don't know

Unfamiliar places

Water

What else are you afraid of?

_____

_____

_____

_____

_____

_____

Sometimes people are embarrassed about being afraid.

Are you embarrassed about being afraid? You don't need to be.

Why?

Because everybody in the world is afraid sometimes.

You are a person, and because you are . . .

you will sometimes experience fear.

Fear is an emotion that makes people feel uncomfortable.

But sometimes fear makes a person do something that needs to be done.

Pretending you're not afraid, so other people will think you are big and brave, is not a good way to handle your fear.

It's important to pay attention to your fear, because it might be a warning that you are in danger.

The best way to handle your fears is to admit you are afraid and be careful.

You can also tell someone else about what you are afraid of. Ask
questions about your fears and find out about them.

You might find out you don't need to be afraid.

Or, you might find out you're right to be afraid. **51**

Remember:

It's OK to be afraid of things that you don't understand and things that might hurt you.

It's also OK to want to get away and hide from things that scare you.

But when you're afraid, don't pretend you're not afraid.

The best things to do are:

Pay attention to your fear.

Remember that fear can be a warning that you're in danger.

Admit that you are afraid.

Be careful.

Tell someone else about your fear.

Ask questions and find out about the things that scare you.

Knowing and remembering these things about fear will help you cope with dangerous things, places, and situations.

Chapter 2

Dangerous Things

Things that could harm you or someone else are dangerous.

Aerosol and spray cans can be dangerous if they are not used wisely and properly. If the contents are sprayed into someone's eyes, ears, nose or mouth, they could harm him or her. Also, aerosol cans explode if they get too hot.

Chemicals, such as medicines and cleaning products, can be dangerous if they are not used wisely and properly. Some chemicals can make you very sick and even kill you, if you swallow them. Other chemicals can hurt your skin, if they get on you.

Kitchen utensils, such as knives, can be dangerous if they are not used wisely and properly. They can cut you or prick you badly.

Razors can be dangerous when they are not used wisely and properly. Since razor blades are very sharp, they can cut you badly and make you bleed a lot.

Recreational equipment, such as slingshots, darts, and archery sets, can be dangerous when they are not used wisely and safely. These things can injure you and even cut off part of your body or poke out your eyes.

Electrical appliances can be dangerous if they are not used wisely and properly. If you are wet or standing in water when you plug in an electrical appliance, you might get a terrible shock.

Putting things other than a plug into an electrical outlet can also make you get a shock.

Tools can be dangerous if they are not used wisely and properly. If you aren't careful when you use tools, you might cut or bruise yourself badly. You might even cut off part of your body.

Hand tools, such as axes, hammers, saws, and screwdrivers can be dangerous. . .

ONCE, WHEN I WAS YOUR AGE, I ALMOST CUT OFF MY FINGER WHEN I WAS USING A JIGSAW. I WASN'T THINKING ABOUT WHAT I WAS DOING.

but power tools, such as electric saws, sanders, and drills, can be even more dangerous. Like all electrical appliances, they can give you a bad shock if they are not used wisely and properly.

Fire can be dangerous if it is not used wisely and properly. It can damage or destroy things, and hurt or kill people.

Explosives, such as firecrackers, can be dangerous if they are not used wisely and properly. An explosive that blows up too close to you might make you blind or deaf. It might also burn you or blow off part of your body.

Guns can be dangerous if they are not used wisely and properly. A gunshot wound can cripple you, blow off part of your body, or even kill you.

All these things are dangerous:

>Aerosol and spray cans.
>
>Chemicals.
>
>Knives and other kitchen utensils.
>
>Razors.
>
>Recreational equipment.
>
>Electrical appliances.
>
>Tools.
>
>Fire.
>
>Explosives.
>
>Guns.

These things are dangerous—but they are also interesting.

Because dangerous things are interesting, children are often curious about them and want to experiment with them.

Would you like to know more about dangerous things? Would you like to experiment with them?

It's OK to be curious about things you don't know about.

It's also OK to want to experiment with things that might be dangerous.

But before you experiment with something that can be dangerous . . .

You need to be strong enough.

You also need to be smart enough. To be safe, ask your
parents to help you decide if you are strong enough and
smart enough to handle a dangerous thing.

75

If you are strong enough and smart enough to handle the thing you want to use, you need to learn how to use it safely and properly.

ANY TIME YOU USE A JIGSAW, YOU SHOULD WEAR SOMETHING TO PROTECT YOUR EYES. AND BE CAREFUL TO KEEP YOUR HANDS AWAY FROM THE BLADE.

You must use the dangerous thing only to do what it's meant to do.

Make sure an adult is nearby when you use a dangerous thing, and be sure the adult knows what you're doing.

Remember, before you use a dangerous thing:

> be sure you are strong enough and smart enough to handle it,
> learn how to use it safely and properly,
> use it only for what it's meant to do,
> make sure an adult is nearby when you are using it, and
> be sure the adult knows what you are doing.

If you use dangerous things wisely and properly, you will not hurt yourself or other people.

Chapter 3

Dangerous Places

Places where you or someone else could get hurt are dangerous.

Animal enclosures, such as cages, corrals, and fenced-in areas, can be dangerous places. If you went inside, the animals might hurt you.

Animal trails can be dangerous places to walk. If you get in the way of the animals, you might get hurt by them.

HORSEBACK RIDING TRAIL
FOR HORSEBACK RIDING ONLY!

<u>Caves</u> can be dangerous places to explore. Because it's dark inside, it is hard to tell what is in the cave. There might be wild animals inside that could hurt you. There might also be wet places or jagged rocks that you should stay away from.

Driveways and parking lots can be dangerous places to play, because if you get in the way of a car, truck, or motorcycle you could get hurt.

High places, such as the tops of buildings, can be dangerous places. If you fall off, you could get hurt badly.

Enclosed spaces that don't have airholes, such as the insides of closets, refrigerators, and freezers, are dangerous. They have only enough air for you to breathe for a short time. When the air is all used up, you might die.

TOMMY WOULD NEVER FIND ME IN HERE! THE TROUBLE IS, I'D PROBABLY RUN OUT OF AIR AND SUFFOCATE.

Big holes in the ground are dangerous to play around, because if you accidentally fall into one, you might have a very hard time getting out again.

Bodies of water, such as lakes, ponds, pools, rivers, and fast streams, can be dangerous if you can't swim and don't have a good strong life jacket or raft.

<u>Polluted</u> areas, where there is a lot of smoke, dirt, and grime in the air and on the ground, can be bad for your health. Being around these areas too long can make you very sick.

91

Places where large machines are stored can be dangerous. If you get too close to the machines while they are running, they could hurt or even kill you.

Unexplored or uninhabited areas can be dangerous, because it's hard to know what's there. You might find wild animals, swamps, steep cliffs, poisonous plants, or sharp thorns that could hurt you.

Streets and highways can be dangerous places. If you play or walk on them, you might get hurt by the cars and trucks.

All these places are dangerous:

> Animal enclosures.
>
> Animal trails.
>
> Caves.
>
> Driveways and parking lots.
>
> High places.
>
> Enclosed places.
>
> Big holes in the ground.
>
> Bodies of water.
>
> Polluted areas.
>
> Places where large machines are stored.
>
> Unexplored, uninhabited areas.
>
> Streets and highways.

These places are dangerous, but they can also be fascinating. Playing around them can be a lot of fun.

Would you like to play around any of these areas?

Would you like to know more about the dangerous places around you? Would you like to explore them and play around them?

It's OK for you to be curious about dangerous places.

It's OK for you to want to play in areas that might be dangerous.

But before you explore a dangerous area . . .

Get an adult to go with you.

With the adult, inspect the dangerous area carefully.

Ask the adult to explain what is dangerous about the area.

STEER CLEAR OF THAT AREA OVER THERE. THE BANK IS PRETTY SLIPPERY THERE AND YOU MIGHT FALL IN. THE WATER IS RUSHING REALLY FAST IN THAT SPOT, AND YOU COULD GET SWEPT AWAY.

Tell the adult about any fears you have, and ask any questions you have about the area.

Listen carefully to the answers the adult gives you.

THAT'S A WATER SPIDER. IT WON'T HURT YOU. YOU DON'T HAVE TO BE AFRAID OF IT.

Promise you won't go near the dangerous area unless an adult is with you or the place is made safe. Then keep your promise.

Remember, before you play in or around a dangerous area:

Always get an adult to go with you.

With the adult, inspect the area carefully.

Ask the adult to explain what is dangerous about the area.

Tell the adult about any fears you have, and ask any questions you have about the area.

Listen carefully to the answers the adult gives you.

Promise you won't go near the dangerous area unless an adult is with you or the place is made safe. Then keep your promise.

If you think before you play around a dangerous area and are careful, you won't get hurt.

Chapter 4

Dangerous Situations

Dangerous situations are things that happen that can hurt you.

Natural phenomena, such as earthquakes, tornadoes, hurricanes, and floods, are dangerous situations.

Man-made disasters, such as fire, accidents, and explosions, are dangerous situations.

Criminal activities, such as robbery, kidnapping, rape, and murder are dangerous situations.

Encounters with wild or unfamiliar animals can be dangerous.

Do you ever think about dangerous situations? Are you afraid some of these things might happen to you?

Natural phenomena, such as earthquakes, tornadoes, hurricanes, and floods.

Man-made disasters, such as fire, accidents, and explosions.

Criminal activities, such as robbery, kidnapping, rape, and murder.

Encounters with wild or unfamiliar animals.

If you are like most people, you hope you never find yourself in a dangerous situation. You probably want to do everything you can to stop them from happening.

It's OK to be afraid of dangerous situations, but no one can stop them from happening.

What you <u>can</u> do is learn all about them so you can avoid them as much as possible and so you will know what to do when you find yourself in one.

Here is how you can learn about dangerous situations.

The first thing you can do is ask questions.

The second thing you can do is research the subject. Talk to people who know about dangerous situations that could happen to you. Read books and magazines, and watch television programs on the subject. And don't stop researching until you know everything you want to know.

Once you understand a dangerous situation, you might be able to keep away from it. And if it does happen to you, you will know what to do to stay as safe as possible.

Conclusion

You are an important person, and because you are . . .

you need to take good care of yourself.

You must not misuse dangerous things.

You must not play carelessly in or around dangerous places.

You must try to avoid dangerous situations and learn how to handle them.

If you understand dangerous things, places, and situations . . .

and if you think before you get involved with them . . .

You will be well on your way to living a long, happy life.